WONDER

By

Henry Hoover

For Ma and Da,

For Chaise and David,

I love you.

And for *you*.

I love you, too.

Dear Reader,

Thank you for reading this book or at least holding it in your hand as you try to decide whether or not you even want to. Written over the course of 4 years, this trilogy documents what can be gained when one loses and what can be lost when one is not willing to try. Starting with Wonder, "Three Mysteries/Three Miracles" is the product of 3 January Firsts, 3 Christmases, 1 February 29th, and 4 birthdays. It is, within itself, an epiphany realized that would not exist without 1,296 days of contemplation and 7 moments or intense agony and bliss. This is a tale about the world: the past, the present, the future, and of course, love; whether you read from cover to cover, or flip to a random page, I sincerely hope you enjoy what's written. Without further ado, I give you Wonder.

Love, Henry

Table of Contents

- See- 6
- It's All Ok- 8
- If- 10
- Long, Lost- 12
- Processes- 13
- Topical T.-15
- Split-Time- 16
- On Your…-17
- Honest...- 18
- Fly Away- 20
- Simple Truths-21
- Paint the…-22
- Everyday- 23
- Something- 24
- Without- 25
- Forget…-26
- Chose- 27
- Pride- 28
- Blood Rhythm- 30
- Worrying- 32
- Light- 33
- Don't/Won't- 34
- Pain is Planted- 35
- With the…- 36
- Good- 37
- Safety- 38
- I Am- 39

- Hold Me Dear- 40
- Tea Leaves- 41
- Autumn…- 42
- Political…- 43
- Frankenstein- 44
- These Days…- 45
- Torn Asunder- 46
- I Had a…-47
- Close Your...-48
- Lack-Thereof- 49
- You Can- 50
- Higher Esteem- 51
- Demands- 53
- Positive…- 56
- Nights That…-57
- I'll Be Ok- 59
- The Change- 60
- Momentous…- 62
- That Feeling- 63
- Bear Down- 64
- Far and…- 65
- 1st Time Lust- 66
- Water-Painted- 68
- So Sweet- 69
- Washes- 70
- Human to…- 71

Table of Contents

- Reach- 72
- Hope Your...-73
- Bruised- 74
- Gentle Eras- 75
- Easier- 76
- Do You...- 77
- Yearn For...- 85
- Minute Hand..-87
- You- 88
- And When...-89
- Seven- 90
- Play Across- 92
- Of Magic- 94
- Heaven- 95
- Future- 98
- I Miss You- 99
- Where Am I?- 102
- Years- 104
- Void- 105
- I Am Yours- 107
- Held High- 108
- Take A...- 111
- I'm Reminded..-112
- Belligerent- 113
- Of You- 115

- Some Days- 119
- Chances...-120
- I Desire- 121
- Drips Heavy- 123
- Albuquerque...- 127
- Anyways- 129

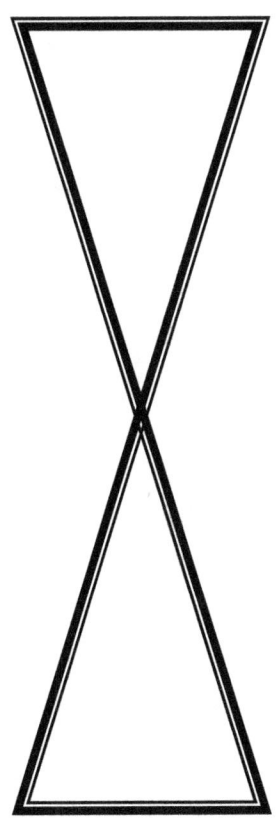

See

Strain to see

Through clouds

So white

Water vapor

Wisps and

Trails

Beyond

All that is known

Deplete, deplete

Then grow

Continue to

Trip on my

Ankles, my

Swinging ankles

I feel soil,

  See

    Soil, ground

    Yet my head

    Is in the clouds

    From time to

    Time I

    See, I

    See you, I

    See me

    Now and then

    It's clear

It's All Ok

Tell yourself it is all ok

But know it to be true

Don't allow the words to

Be hollow, be empty

Constructed only to fill

The void

Believe it to be true

Look to the future

And see gold, look at today

And see gold

Because without this

Priceless ability

All is empty

All is constructed only to fill

The void

It's All Ok

And not to bridge the gap

Between here and there

Now and then

To make it possible

To leave the void

In the past

Tell yourself it's all ok

Right now

Say it aloud

And

Believe it to be true

If

If I had you

By my side

If plans went

Accordingly

Would I be

By your side

Or tucked away

Deep

Hidden

Shelter me, shelter me

Know not your ways

Of error

Shield my body

From your touch

I'll shield yours with mine

If

And as you fade

I'll lose myself

Drifting through days

I'll never be

I never was

Something more than this

And though it's something

I never had

You're someone

Whom I miss

Long, Lost

I seem to always be

To always want

To always need

I seem to always lose myself

In nameless days

And weeks

I take a step forward

But take two steps back

Searching for that

Something

Never knowing

What I'll find

Browsing over

Long, lost pages

Words that are countless

Years old

The truth is I lost myself when I was 11 years of age

Processes

My mind

My mental

Process and patterns

Felt sharp

And overbearing

Now dull

And hardly

Apparent

I feel well

Though ill

Whole though

Lacking

Oh, I want

How I want

To be whole

And well

Light or sharp

Not overbearing

Processes

But not hardly

Apparent, I

Want to shine

And fly

Wings spread high

And, I want you

How I want you

By my side

Topical Topography

I love

Swirling below

Topical topography

Skin moist

Mistakes made

I just don't

Know where

I want to go

Lost with

Nowhere to go

Place myself

Point approach

Mind swimming

Tides changing

And I'm begging

Split-time

By no mistake

I'm on the floor

I've fallen once

More, shoulders

Heavy, question

Days, sunset

Rise

Time doesn't quite

Pursue me, rather,

Peruses me

I will rant and

Rave during those

Days and hold it

Against that time

Looking for more time

Lost time, during those times

I'll come to find that

My time is split-time

On Your Shoulders

You bore on

Your shoulders

Pain for me

Shame for me

You brought

A whirlwind

Across the threshold

Through my

Door and

Further

For free

For me

And now

I'm crying,

Shivering

In cold, dusk

Glory

Waiting to witness new additions

Honest Behavior

Honest behavior

Sun rises

In the East

Or a direction

We all meet

Visually, spiritually

A destination

We strive

To meet

Sky soaring beauty

Stars between

All that lies

Beneath us

And all that

Is unseen

Perpetual dusk

Twilight haze

Guides us

Honest Behavior

Through this

Wandering maze

And leads us

To a place

Far from shore

Far from touch

Only by vessel

Sauntering waves

Can one hope to find

The self

Fly Away

The quickest

Way to

Fly away

Is to find

A sky

Opened wide

Catch the

Breeze

And

Gently

Glide

Simple Truths

If days were to pass

Any slower

Any faster

It would not make

Anything

More bearable

Anything

More unbearable

It would not

It could not

Change my

Simple truths

Paint the Ceiling

My mind needs

Laughter, silence

My mind needs

Disarray

Cloudless days

My mind needs

Tears and rain

My mind needs

Spotless linen, stains

My mind needs

Love, words of love

My mind needs

Walls to hold

Love

My mind needs

My mind needs

Plain and simple

My mind needs

Everyday

Everyday results

In every evening

Being the same

Feeling the same

And every night

Is the product

Of every evening

Being the same

Bearable and tangible

Used to be two separate things

Now, they lay

Side by side

Everyday results

Can result in

Once in a lifetime

Opportunities

If you only know

How to say yes or no

Something

It's not something living

With flesh and blood

But gives life and breath

Opens my eyes

And when I feel it coming

Pulsing amidst

My thoughts and veins

I tense and shudder

Always clenched fists

And uncertainty

It writhes beneath my skin

And forces me to question

To question my future, present, past

My blood stream moves it, guides it

And my body is surrendered

When it's given, when it's taken

My hands slacken, my being calms

And I feel and I know

Without

Effortless like

A cool, warm breeze

Moist upon my skin

Brings in the rain

Brings in the storms

Thunder in lightning

Brings in the rain

And from the calm

From its passing

Without effort

Life conquerors

FORGET

YOURSELF

REMEMBER

YOUR SELF

Chose

Missing him in this strange light

Masks feelings kept unaware

Unbeknownst to its holder and creator

Missing her on this strange day

Forces my being upright, stand guard

My direction is aimless

The world is abound

My cares seem frivolous, though

They pain me to hold

There are some things in

This world I'll never understand

And that I may never have

She will be the North

He will be the South

And I will be caught

In their magnetic web

Tangled by true direction

Pride

Pride, pride will

Stay perhaps

Pride, it may

Stay

But I will

Push, I will

Keep it afar

See it, ajar

My hand

Will remain

Pushing it far

And we will

Avoid

Yes, we will

Avoid

And our pride

Will be dead

Humility

Pride

Won't lead us

Astray

To falter

It will guide us

Gently

It will color us

All

Blue

Blood Rhythm

When heart beats

Beat

With uncertainty

In darkness

Find light

When stale breaths

Are taken

With emptiness

Without care

Find reasons

When thoughts spill

Across blank

Ears, pages, skin

From sorrow/blue

Change processes

Blood Rhythm

And when the

Light is found

When reasons

Are realized

When processes

Reassemble and gravitate

Around

Light and realized reason

Day by day

I'll smile more

Breathe easier

Think of you

Worrying

Worrying

Begets nothing

Becomes everything

Engulfs

And expands

To envelope

Myself entirely

Exponentially

Leads me nowhere

Guides me to desolation

Fills my thoughts

Devours my time

Leaves me

Empty

Light

Light shine

Shine on me

And shine on you

Light just shine

Just shine

And we'll be alright

Always

Some nights, I fear

A new day will never come

Don't/Won't

Leaves on the floor

My memories

Still lying around

Don't complain

Don't speak your transgressions

I won't let it go

Speak your peace

Only if it's peace

Step outside

And gently sigh

But what lies heavy

On my shoulders, wide

Is what I bear

Every second, every minute, every way

Pain Is Planted

If you only, if you could

Yes, I know you, knew you would

Sit still vacant, sit still clear,

Sit there empty, have no fear

It's the world around us, that dirty place

Full of sorrow, full of waste

It brings this feeling to your door

Hurts your kind heart, hurts your core

Makes you hide your face at night

When it seems there is no hope in sight

But let me tell you, you must know

That where pain is planted, pain will grow

So when you look at the world today

And your heart and soul fill with dismay

Please, just know that it can change

That a better tomorrow is just in range

If you see the world for what it is

Then, friend, that means there's hope

With The Ground

Wheels turn

Keep this in motion

Mental and physical

Time knows no boundaries

Time pauses for no one

My mind's eye

Presents these futures

Shows me what's possible

But not where to go

My feet search for places

To step

My heart searching

For truths to accept

These mountains, these valleys

My soul they surround

I'm one with this soil

I'm one with this ground

Water drips and water collects

Good

I could never look back

Always faced forward

But from whence I came

To forget is a risk

I could never dream

Always in the past

But to where I am going

I'd risk never knowing

I could remember neither

Only live now

But who I am, was, and will become

Would be nothing more than a leaf

Floating with the doctrines

Of the eternally changing winds

I'd rather find foot holds

In parts of all three

Where I came from and will go

Where I am

Safety

When thunder

When light plays

Darts

Flows

When silver, purple,

Indigo blues

Flood the sky

Fill the night sky

Listen, just

Stop.

Listen.

See, hear, smell,

Taste, stop,

Listen.

Begin or end

Stop, listen.

I Am

I am lost

I am alone

I am empty

I am abandoned

I am hurting

I am yearning

I am begging

I am screaming

I am crying

I am searching

I am on my knees

I am pleading

I am dying

I am dying

Hold Me Dear

Hide and seek

Hidden amongst the leaves

I find my scattered dreams

I lean down and search

My knees

Gripping and grinding

Gravity holds me

Holds me dear

Reflections send me running

But hold

What I know true

And if I could separate dissipate

From this

Soulless cloud

I could see myself

Again, my

Dreams

Again

Tea Leaves

Tomorrow is a day

One could only predict

In tea leaves

Looking down

At tea leaves

His hand reaches

Down, today and

Tomorrow

It's up to you to see

In cloudless skies

And stars so bright

He's waiting there for me

But me, I'm weak

Me, I'm lowly

I tremble at his touch

And when I fall

I lay there

I just lay there

Autumn/Summer Heat

If the rain

Could make

My vision moist

Palpable in this

Autumn fire

Then the silence

Can make

My breath stale

As the summer wind

Blowing against your leaves

You can hold me

But only for so long

Political Process

This political process

Alarmingly obscure

You think you understand it

But

If monsters are created,

Not born,

Who are the monsters?

Frankenstein

Pitfalls hold me

Fall before me

And I can't save myself

My thoughts are storming

Raining down

And God it's hard to see

My true direction

Yes, once I knew

But you never wanted me

To succeed

Just one step

Forward or behind

Regardless of location

My future

Rests on surface tension

And watching families in the woods

Reading their books

Finding myself in arctic places

These Days Are Now

How many summers

Must one have

How many years to be

How many paths

Must one have taken

How many paths to envision

I feel this thunder

This vibration, true

Of days soon to come

I feel this current

It's pulsing through my core

Pushing me to these days

To these days to come

And blessed light falls

Upon my face, warming heart and soul

And now I know

And now I feel

I feel, heart and soul

Torn Asunder

Time lingers

Nails dig in

Deep

Penetrates our

Skin

Looking over

Now and then

Heaven and

Earth

Begin to spin

Torn asunder

Heart beats quicken

I Had a Dream

I had a dream last night

There was fear all around me

This dream felt real, this dream stayed with me

Will be with me forever, I believe

There was a boy

In my dream, there was a boy

And oh how the boy was to grow

Or so they said

But he fell through the ice instead

Momentary loss of self

He fell through the ice instead

And all of the eyes standing around

Not one helping hand

Reached down

In my dream

There was a boy

And oh how he started to drown

CLOSE YOUR EYES

Lack Thereof

No oxygen

No room to breathe

Forgetting the feel of sunlight

Forgetting the blue sky

Memories erased

You mustn't worry

Uniform and scheduled

Plan out your day

Pills of all shapes

Alter your reality

What am I missing?

What am I not feeling,

Not remembering?

Nothing

I am home

You Can

If you can

If you can't

Only make sure

Promise

That it is your

Decision

Not some trifle

Of words that just happened

To slip out

Of some stranger's pursed, dry lips

Of course

Before you decide

Whether you can

Or can't

Remember and know

Truly know

That you

Can

Higher Esteem

Do you know

At times

Those times

When you sway

To and fro

Do you know

The pain you

Cause?

For to be

True or to

Be wrong

Is better

Than to know

And then change, then

You know only

To change

But rather it is in

Higher esteem

Higher Esteem

To know

And to grow

You can know

And be wrong or right

But wait

To find out

Before you

Allow yourself

To be wavering

Like the ocean's surface

Like the cloudless

Sky by night

And storm by

Day, act your

Part, know your

Ways, and above

All else, allow

Yourself benefit

Of the doubt

Benefit. Of. The. Doubt.

Demands

Your open

Hand

Demands

In my mind

In my heart

I see through

You

Or think I

Do

And I want

I have come

To want

And it hurts

And I'm hurt

For what

What if

My truths

Have come

Demands

Undone

Believing

Flippant revelations

Falsely perceived

Communications

But I do

I believe

I honestly

Believe

I'm sorry

To tell you

I'm sorry

To say

Sorry for

You

For you

Don't deserve

My mountains

My oceans

Lack of discipline

Demands

Yet, in the end

I've changed

For you

No

In your light

I've changed

And

I'm trying

Positive/Negative

I'm not positive

All of the time

And perhaps that

Is my personal detriment

My personal pain

I am positive

At times and

For me

It is uplifting

When I am positive

I am not always

Certain and

I'm trying to

I'm going to

I'm trying to find the truth

Know the truth

Be positive and certain

Every single day

Nights That Save

Not knowing,

Thinking, believing

Mentally seeing

Sure, but

Not knowing

Is heavy

Some days

I think i

Know

Others, I know I

Know

Then there are days

Days that burn

Days that pour

Days that force

Me to question

How much I

Truly know

Nights That Save

Then there are nights

Nights that save

Nights that nourish

Nights that remind

And it is

Truly

Those nights

That lead to days that

Save, nourish, remind

I'll Be Ok

Can you be scared, be frightened

With me

Can you move forward but not know where

To be

Can you look up and down

And see nothing

If not

Can you see it all

Can you call me by a name

That belongs to no one

Can you find me

In a place

That isn't

Here

Can you move forward

Without me

I'll be ok

I'll be ok

The Change

Stars shine down

Cast ancient light

Worldly emissions

Prophetic submissions

At a remove

So just stand still

It's always turning

This mass beneath

Our feet

Reflections are

Projected three

Hundred and sixty degrees

Even in the pitch

Of night

Sometimes they are

The Change

Captured

These vain representations

And held for

Seconds in a

Passing, moving

Car window/door

And somewhere

They are heard

With fire

And someone

Wields the words

With fervor

The spark

To make

The change

On slabs of concrete

Cracked grey floor

Green grass grows

Moving for

An ancient light

Momentous Improvisation

Your actions depict the

Restrictions your

Mind's eye holds

And design the

Path your feet

May follow

Words and hallowed

Moments of glory

Glorious realization

Momentous improvisation

Stay far from

Black clouds

Stray far from

Dark thoughts

Actualize dreams

Hopes, sought

After stories

To disclose

That Feeling

Moments to use

Congruent and

Opening my eyes

Only light surrounds

This time is nothing more than a sliver

Of all that could enfold,

Envelope, hold

Moments that fill

Hot, beat racing

Cause your hands

To shake, shake

Shake, already

Breathing is cut short

Progression on creation

The statements remain the same

Progression, creation

They share each other's life force

Are each other's fool

Bear Down

Hold on to

Thoughts, hold on

To short structured

Strokes, blending

Colors, one by one

Eyes closed

Remote thoughts

Pull forward

Remote places

I've yet to

Explore

Long lost

Smiles hurt

Bear down

Far and In-between

To everyone, someone

To everyone, something

To you or me

Find it

Deep

To you or me

To hold

I ask

For more

Than goes

To him or her

What is spread

Far and

In-between

I ask for more

Than what is found

To be few

And far between

First Time Lust

Something afar

Outlined

But not known

Wanted

But not needed

Like everything else

Like nothing ever

Witnessed

Collective or

Draining

Lust fills

My heart

And the world

Is on mute

Convulsions of

Desire

Unknown to

Myself

First Time Lust

Unheard of

To myself

Reverberate

Throughout

My body

My husk

This guise

I need you now

More than ever

I know this now

More than ever

Water-Painted Green

Day light silver

Moonlit glow

Grey, pale skies

Above, throughout

Water-painted green

Tree branches sway

Warm breeze, warm rhythms

Savage without care

Sudden seduction catches my eye

Water painted trees

Their leaves hold my stare

Then bathroom floor, tile dry

The ceiling spins

Fingers grip the tile floor and sink

Day light silver

Whispers, calling

Moonlit glow

Crooning so soft, so slow

So Sweet

Separate

Trudge through

What you know to be dead weight

Separate

All that's gold

And glitter

Silver shine so sweet

Resonate

With silent rooms

Dust floating

Amongst white light

Separate

Meditate

Mediate

Shadows fade, illuminate

All that will be done

All that draws so near

All becomes clear

Washes

Friendly shine

Direction known

Foot-steps follow

Thoughts

Bruised and blistered

Worn and tired

Heart beats

Through the drought

Rain comes, washes

Away any pain

Left behind

Human to More

Scream

Triumph or terror

Neither here

Nor there

Heart rate quickens

Blood boils, thickens

Thoughts race like

Words

Feel soul, feel

Light

Feel angel feathers

Surround

Grimace, twist and toil

Always time later

To recoil

Transition from

Human to more

Transition from human to something more

Reach

Everything apparent and beautiful

Lies inches beyond my reach

My grip

Which lately

To be honest

Started to slip

So where will

My footsteps lead

Or am I moving

And if I trust

I've set sail

Just what am

I supposed to do

And when my world shakes

I stumble

Should I

Trust it is

All ok?

Hope Your World

Empty and dreary

Waning spirits

Fail to lift

Feet far from

The ground

Morning minutes

Seconds linger

To look around

Hope your world

Softly, despairingly

Falls into

Open hands

Willing life

Grasp

I hope

To all end

For salvaged breath

Bruised

Bruised

I am bruised

And hurt

Breathing short, still

Face, shoulders

Shudder, sporadic

Drawn out thoughts

Hands with hair

Tied between

Pulling, covering

Ears, drowning

Out noise

Heart beats quick, fast

Shimmer, help.

You're where?

Hands reaching down

Are where?

And myself?

Gentle Eras

Subtle

Gentle eras

Revisited

Want to

Transform

Daylight

Found

Face forward

Two people

Should not

Fight

Two nations

Or more

Should never go to war

Yet they do

We do

Fast flight

I prefer a gentle area I visited

Easier

New friends and faces

Easier to breathe

Easier to smile

Easier

Old faces and friends

I know them

Remember them

Oh so well

Directions, directions

Feeling lost

And found

Truly profound

New friends and faces

Same old sigh

Same old desire

Do You Want To Know The Truth?

I'm sorry

The truth is

I'm sorry

In disarray

Scatter, shocked

Thoughts sporadic

And clean

Wind caresses

Undressed my

Mind elated

Truth remains

To me unseen

At night, however

Do You Want To Know The Truth

Slack jaw

Cold sweat

I know

At night, however

My independence

Iron spine'd, steel framed

Golden torso'd, silver shouldered

In darkness

Mind's eye bright

My inner dependence

Comes undone

Fail to understand

I come undone

Unwind, unbind

I appear as one

But fall apart

Do you want to

Know the truth?

Do You Want To Know The Truth

Thoughts of you

Appear unclear

At first, in red

Or blue

Sorrowfully, I'll say

It's true

My thoughts, they drift

To you

My thoughts

At times, yes

They are of you.

I keep myself

40 feet away

Arms out

They must

Stay clear

And in the morning

Mirror shine

Do You Want To Know The Truth

It is only me

I see

And in my bed

Beneath my

Blankets, pillows too,

You race across

My mind

Blazoned in blue

Front and torso, too

Blazoned in blue

But my bed only

Knows my weight,

Shape, the way

I've been since

Young

The way I'll

Be so soon

To come

I'm only known

As one

Do You Want To Know The Truth

The truth

Spills down

My shepherd's

Calf

From noon 'til

Half past four

Time for slaughter

Forever more

The flesh keeps

Our souls free

At times,

However,

Namely,

Night,

The ground beneath

Me quakes

If I'm enveloped

By a dream

Do You Want To Know The Truth

I find myself awake

And two

In the morning

'Til half past four

My soul once

Free, now sure,

I fear, at

Times, you'll

Reappear, yes,

In my core

My heart

Emblazoned

With you

And the truth

Is like moths,

Humans are

Attracted to light

And it's

The flame reflected

Do You Want To Know The Truth

In your eyes

That, for me,

Glows most bright

The truth is

I've learned

A lot about

Building walls

From words

But walls mean

Nothing to

The dove or

Any other bird

No, walls mean

Nothing to the dove

Or one that

Is submerged

Do You Want To Know The Truth

Whether, like a dove,

You've found your place

By flying high above

Or burrowed beneath

The wall untouched

In my heart

You sink your teeth

My knees tremble

My walls fall down

I take a second look

The truth is

That you took

My guarded heart

From its cage

Yearn For Release

I can't do this

I thought I would

Or could but

Worn and pain

Ridden, lacking

Sleep and a golden

Splendor that my

Whole world once

Would keep

Now vanished

Has pushed me

To edges previously unknown

To return

I burn

Yearn for release and

Dreams entangle

Me or lie

With soft lullabies

Yearn For Release

Of truths

That act

Only as proof

For the amount

Of worthlessness

I do hold

Ideas, goals

Rot in outstretched

Hands, as I

Wait for one

Miracle to behold

Only you

Can save me

Forgive me

Wash me of my

Disgusting form

Only you

Know me, I'll allow

To control me, and

Please do

Minute Hand Ribs

Time almost hurts

It pushes your

Shoulders

Jabs your ribs

From the moment

You are born

Until the moment you are dying

It hurries you

Without warning

Without caution

It quickens you

Until you understand

Until you can run ahead

Look o'er your shoulder

Time is not to be found

Look to your side

And time

Is running with you

You

Touch and go

Look both ways

Whilst crossing

The street

Freshen up

Before

You never know

Who you might

Meet

You never know

What lies ahead

Lay

Yourself down in bed

And realize, day

By day

You make it all

The same

And When I'm Clean, I'll Come Back; I Always Loved You

I couldn't tell you

All those things

All of those lovely things

Like

Your smile, how

I love your smile

And the smell, how

I love the smell of your neck

And your deliberate

Laughter at jokes

Of mine that

Simply aren't funny

And you, how

I love you

Seven

7 years of age

Pressed against

White porcelain

This won't

Hurt a bit…

Years later

Years later

This will cost

You

Therapy, time

Pills and friends

Self-medicate

Self-deprecate

Now you're 12

12 years of age

Now

This may hurt

Seven

You

More, don't cry

Hand over your

Mouth, don't cry

Years later

Years later

This may stay

In the mirror

At your bedside

Table, muffled conversation

Muffled sobs

Don't cry

Play Across

Don't detract

Refract

Take something back

Do look so far in

That vessels and time

Are tiny games

That you play in your

Head while bored

Wonderful things

Delight and shudder

Play across your mind

Colors spinning

Its music filling your

Ears and it all becomes so

Apparent, you

Only have to

Count the years

Months, weeks,

Play Across

Days, both

Slowly and quickly

Do the hours streak

By and by lending

Only these visions soon

To come dancing

And swirling and playing

In your being

Of Magic

There once was a time

Of magic, life was full

And then, all at once

The magic ceased to be

I would awaken everyday

Darkness would turn to light

But the darkness it would stay

Hidden deep

Hurting deep

Painful deep inside

Don't hurt me, leave early

There once was a time

Of magic, life was full

And then, all at once

The magic ceased to be

Empty glasses of wine

Seemed to fill our time

And the days and weeks would pass

Heaven

You are in the present

Perfect tense

The line fades and blurs

Twists and tumbles

Between now and then

Heaven

Heart beats quicken

Floating into gravity

Sparks fly when I touch

When you touch

Cascading into a summer storm

Feel the electricity

Pulsing, always pulsing

Eyes closed and falling

Never have I seen, felt

Happiness so vivid

Trace my smile with

Your fingers and smile

Heaven

Because I smile

Thankful to see your eyes

A kindness never before known

Everything about you

Never before known

Your midnight kiss

On moonlit streets bathed in silver

And glowing, I feel

Your warmth against

My warmth

A brilliant and beautiful

Color

Our innocence

And time stands still

For us, only for us

As white feathers surround

We can't help but laugh

As we try to catch them

Steal them from grace

All becomes quiet

Heaven

Save our rhythmic breathing

Our eyes locked

In a kaleidoscope we embrace

Radiating, you feel it now

Once undetected, but now you know

Seeing it in my eyes

Tasting it on my lips

Staining and painting each fallen feather

This brilliant and beautiful color

Our innocence

Future

Hazy, I struggle

Though temporary

Too few and far between

Puzzle pieces engulfed

In grey matter and

Scar tissue, calcium

Deposits yearning to heal

To discern which

Way to go, turn

Away from past

Times and memories

Thinking on the porch

And something drifts

Ashore, for a moment that is

Complete, enrapture grammar, words,

Thoughts, still shots of humid

Last days, gatherings

Not likely to be seen again

I Miss You

I saw you

The other day

You were vines

Greener than I

Had ever seen before

Or possibly and simply

More full of life

I saw you in

The trees, our sky

Human nature sprawled

Across my helping

Hands human behavior

Building my grave

For rest, but

When I saw you

My jaw was dropped

Your leaves like emeralds

I saw you in the soil

I Miss You

And later in the stars

I wept for you

Just the other day

I was no where

To be found, and

My feet were leading

Me far away, they lead

Me farther still

I wept because

You were never in

The vines, or in the

Trees, neither in the soil

Nor the stars

And I knew then

I was alone

You were not

In the sky

When I thought

You had heard

My cries, and

I Miss You

Human exposure

Made me feel

Ill, I thought

Of my future

Today, I fear

My own demise

Woven together

By my fingers

They move like spiders

My end is no death

But a momentary

Loss of will, and I

Do this when I lose

Love

Where am I?

When you go

To places

Dark and cold

Swim to places

Of high height

Challenge all

That is

Inside

Outside, scramble

Scatter

Put together

Again

When you look in

The mirror

Stop and listen

Sink and sigh

Lies heavy

Scarring

Where Am I

Stay light

In flight

When you start

To question

Here and there

And everything in-between

Go inside

Through ribs

Of bone

Go deep inside

You're home

Venus

My dear Venus, do you remember

When we had wonder, we had this gold

We would play with fire using our bare hands

Ignore the love that was foretold

Starry nights, they plague my mind

Some days the smoke is thick

My thoughts they bring me

To that hidden place

And then leave me just as quick

Now, I know it's not your fault

And Lord knows it's not mine

But by this alone, we can't save ourselves

From these rips in time

And I still remember our apologies

All of your sweet, soft-spoken words

When, under blue skies, I watch

Just lay and watch the birds

Void

Slipping away

I can feel

Close my eyes

And shhh

Finger to the mouth

And shhh

It's endless

This feeling

Losing myself

Within it

A chasm I've created

A monster at bay

But how much longer

Will it last

When will the beast

Devour me

When will I immerse

Myself

Void

In this wonder

In these questions

This longing and desire

This pain

I want out

I want away

Seconds, minutes, hours

Days, weeks, months

Years

I want out

I want away

Perhaps the path

Lies in the void

I Am Yours

I love you

Or so the

Feeling grows

Grew green grass

Amongst shady groves

Time spent among

Others less set

A river of time

Rushes against

Your shores

And tell me

Which step to take, oh

I'm yours

Yes, I'm yours

Tell me which

Path to trek

Down now, for

I am yours, yes, I am yours

Held High

Misery

Remember me

When your

Time has

Passed, I

No longer wish

To wrap my

Self in your

Disgrace,

Disdain

I no longer

Desire your

Darkest fires

Lighting up

My life

My core hurts

No, worse,

Molten stone

Held High

Burns my flesh

From rib cage

To surface skin

Know, though,

I know too

Much of

My ways

Have changed

I need

To recuperate

I need to

Be select

I cannot

Grow within

This bubble

Thriving is

A form far

Off, I

Hold my

Intentions

Held High

Though lacking

Conviction

Close to my

Muscular

Pump

I hold

My conviction

Lacking intention

In outreached

Hands held

High

TAKE A

DEEP

BREATH

I'm Reminded of Those Hospital Sheets

Hospital sheets

Blindingly white

Unbearably clean

Cold, pale lights

Shine down

Losing my self

In every stitch

Pulling my hair

Scratching that itch

Closed eyes

Fingers grasp

The unknown

And in good supply

Skin on bone

Cold, pale lights

Shine down

Belligerent

I am

Nothing

Something more

Than you

You are cold

And distant

I am hot

Like fire

I burn

And lash out

But I am nothing

Something more

Than you

You see me

You are looking through

You are seeing something

Less than you

But hear me

Belligerent

I am nothing

Something more

Something less

Do not compare me

Do not judge me

I am

Nothing

Something more

Than you

Of You

And I'm stuck between

Faces unseen

With words

I held so true

Over speeding cars

I look at the stars

Thinking thoughts of you

I say that I'm lost

Never knowing the cost

Or where

I'll wind up next

And I've been alone

Like a sitting stone

But baby you've got me vexed

Of You

Fact and fiction

Will sharpen my diction

Though

My questions are unresolved

In our small world

Just water and swirls

I'll wait until we evolve

They say I was jaded

Yeah, I was almost persuaded

But you

Can't trust a single word

Because this fact and fiction

Yeah, it's my affliction

My mind and memory blurred

My heart, it was heavy

Built like a levee

Of You

I was good

At keeping others away

Yet, you've gained admittance

And I've paid my remittance

Yeah baby, I'm here to stay.

I can't say I know you

No, I can't say I do

But maybe

That will change over time

See, I've been broken

Softly outspoken

By mountains impossible to climb

But now I look in the mirror

And it's never been clearer

I can see

Each and every scar

Of You

Of pain I keep hidden

Of loves I've forbidden

I remain cut up and marred

But this, it won't stop me

And you haven't caught me in my

Distant and diluted desire

I'm undeserving

But also unswerving

Secretly, I embrace this fire

And over speeding cars

I look at the stars

Thinking thoughts of you

Yes, on quiet nights,

The stars so bright

I'm thinking thoughts of you

Some Days

It's hard to eat

Some days

It's hard to think

Sleep

Walk and talk

Some days

I want to disappear

Here's to one day

Chances by the Second

Second chance

Like happenstance

I take another breath

Faster now

But knowing how

To take another step

The sun still rises

From the East

And settles in the West

I'll rise with it,

Yes, I'm ready

And when it sets I'll rest.

I Desire

I wish I could drift into the Earth

Become the roots

Which are grounded

Which have been grounded

This will be grounded

I wish I could drift into the sea

And every wound

In you which you inflict

In which I inflict,

Seconds later

Appear non-existent

I wish I could blow with the leaves

And twist

And tumble

And dance with the wind

I Desire

I wish I could be quiet and calm

Remain untouched

Unseen

I would be the foam

Traveling atop waves,

Splitting only for your bow

I would be the air we breathe

Inhale

Exhale

I would be the blades of grass

Glinting with morning dew

I wish I could shed my exterior

To reveal my interior

I wish I could be away

Drips Heavy

Push yourself into a corner

The only thing left to do

Take a look around

Take a look around

Is this what you asked for

Is this what you wanted

Are you miles away from anything

Familiar

And feeling alone

Liar

Are you driving yourself into

The dirt

And slowly losing faith

In this and that

Drips Heavy

The pain drips heavy

The fear has sprung lose

And your heart

Can only palpitate

For so much longer

Before

It bursts

Scream quietly

Silently

Into your pillow

But don't awaken your neighbors

Don't awaken your demons

Just lose faith

In this or that

Here and there

Become stagnant

Drips Heavy

Gather dust like years

Become dust

Over the years

You were once so lively

So full of life

And now you're sinking

Below the water line

Don't breathe in

Don't breathe in

Hold your breathe

But

Do

Not

Breathe

In

Light trickling through

The waves

Sound trickling through the light

Drips Heavy

Get up, just get up

Breathe in.

Breathe in.

Breathe in.

Breathe in.

Is this what you asked for?

Is this what you wanted?

If the answer is no,

If your answer is no.

En Oh

Get out of your corner

Get out of the dirt

Quit soaking in the tub

Quit soaking and smoking

Both cause wrinkles

And make a fucking change

Albuquerque, N.M.

It wasn't the helium balloons that caught me

I wasn't tangled within their strands of string

Or standing in a basket below all of that hot air

The whole of the desert was painted

For you and I

Was the thought

That streamed across my mind

Eli's mother, her girlfriend

Let us sleep in her home

I blushed for

Forty-eight hours

It never felt the same

I laid in the grass, counting

The rainbow of balloons

Albuquerque, N.M.

Wanting to buy us

A ride

I didn't have enough

I wanted to see the orange and pink

The color of corn and green streaks

Fly over that mountain range

They were the first you had ever seen

I wanted to look at Earth

With you

I blushed for forty-eight hours

And twelve more on the drive home

I've never felt the same

Anyways

Fireworks, spring sky grey, but growing

Impregnated with snow, the sparks glowing

Tidal waves rush in reverse, earthquakes

Bring progress and tighter bonds

All is in its place

Stumble, stubborn words and thoughts

Without event, trickle down, down, down

And further still, this current fades

In succession, a recession of all

Those happy dreams like smile lines

That played across your face, disillusioned

And laughter is far off, emblazoned

Upon common-place objects, buried

Beneath the sands of time, there is

No such thing as "mine", and you'd be

Whoever's for the cost of a dime, in

Anyways

Some other place surrounded by other faces

You push the reaching hands away, further away, meditating on love

And other childhood fairy tales of gold

Dust and glitter's splendor

It was never

Easy for me, I kneel to pray but

Forget those words I never learned

And try to remember your eyes for

The sake of solace and inner peace

A stillness so sweet, but find they're

Gazing upon another or somewhere other

Than me

Not that it ever mattered anyways

My pride lies in my strength that

Endures the hail storm and tornado's toil

But crumbles at the sound of your whispered words

Fall too many times and you'll learn to stand

Anyways

Look over your shoulder only to see that you're

Alone and you'll learn to never look again

And how many people were born today

Anyways? Connected consciousness with barriers

Of petty crime and land mines, I

Still remember the way you smelled, that

Day I had all that weight upon my

Shoulders, you helped carry my cross or

Whatever it was that "they" called it, but

I sleep better now, and tend to walk only one way

There's war on TV everyday

The haze of bombs blowing up

Shines on a child's face

It was never supposed to be this way

But how do 8 billion people change?

Your bombs, I realize, were only

In my mind, imagined pit falls, created to

Bear me down, but I'm better now

And I really don't care

Anyways

It was all just in my head or so I've come to learn

But I really, really don't care, and this

Is all just practice for those times to follow

So I'll play dumb and forget all that

Passed me by, the businessmen will

Rape and pillage followed by whiskey

Or beer, the Earth will shatter a little more each day,

But will continue to offer all that He, She has

To offer, hold, and I'll remember

The time the grass was green, bathing

In simplicity, I'll remember streams

Winding as far as the eye could see, pure

And clear, begging us to be like water

We're made of the stuff, anyways

www.ingramcontent.com/pod-product-compliance
Lightning Source LLC
Chambersburg PA
CBHW071516040426
42444CB00008B/1666